A Song For Midnight

by
Heather Blank

ISBN: 9781093539172

Cover Art by
Jody Pham
www.jodypham.com

"I paint my own reality. The only thing I know is that I paint because I need to, and I paint whatever passes through my head without any other consideration."
– Frida Kahlo

MIDNIGHT

An ocean of oxygen
And I am suffocating
I am paralyzed in wilted moonlight.
Everything is monotonous sound,
Nothing more
Than a vitriolic hum—
A song for midnight
And this litter of thoughts.

TROUSERS

All the boys talk over you.
All the boys say the same thing you said first,
But the crowd only hears it in baritone.
All the boys are in bands,
All the boys write poems for women
And they swim in seas of dropped panties.
All the boys paint, and are photographers,
Directors,
And we will stand like doe-eyed sheep in a herd
To appreciate
Their art
It is no wonder women changed their names to write
their deepest desires.
It is no wonder Greta and Marlene wore trousers.

OINTMENT

I was bitter.
I smirked and guffawed in contempt.
I drank until I was cross-eyed,
I cried until my eyes stung.
It is poison.
You have to make yourself raw,
See your own blood.
You have to apply the ointment
To allow the scab to grow,
The skin to grow over, to heal.
And then you come out on the other side.

THE FAVOR

"that picture is so good
it doesn't even look like you"
"you'd be so much prettier
if you wore color"
"why do you wear
so much makeup"
If I just lost
x number of pounds
my life will have
worth and meaning
people will
love me more
people will
hunt me more
even though while I am
F A T
I have to look over
my shoulder
my keys out
between my fingers
why do you do that
no one wants to fuck you
except they do

when they follow me
from the toilet paper aisle
to the hand soap
in the grocery store
asking my relationship status
or if my boyfriend will
let me have a friend
or if my boyfriend
will marry me
because
HE WILL
and if I don't want
to marry him
or to have a friend
aside from my boyfriend
then
fuck you
fat bitch
you're
ugly
anyway
I was doing you
a favor.

SINKING

There is no innocence.
Your calm is disrupted.
I am set out to sea with no note.
An empty bottle.
Each wave fills me deeper,
Salt water sinking,
Weighing me down,
Tears down to the ocean floor.

SHORTCOMINGS

She is
Too smart
Too fat
Too emotional
She speaks
Too cautiously
Too much
Or
Not enough
Punctuated by
Red lipstick
She laughs
Like a hyena
At your expense
Bats her
Long black lashes
Then
Her hand
Slides inside your pants
You accept
Her shortcomings

VOLCANO

It is boiling like a quiet volcano in Iceland.
Near you, I am fire. My insides are melting.
Lava fountains burying this cold rock.
Breath unsteady and nerves sharp against
My heart, tiny knives, I wait, drenched in heat,
In anticipation.
I feel the tickle of the hair on your arm
Against mine and shiver silently.
I will not run for safety.

SPY

I write secret things,
Spy with my thighs
My soul sniffs you out.
I welcome troubled ways,
Kiss anguished lips,
Hot with despair and pout.

CANDY

Every day I think
I either need to move
To Los Angeles, or somewhere
Silent with stars
Every day I pine for coffee
And this stupid heat that I hate
My petunias that I am slowly killing off
I am looking for kindness in every kind of soil
{s o u l}
I am looking for heartbeats that are filled to the brim
My eyes are becoming sore with incessant scouring;
My heart is drying like candy you can eat.

WISER

If I were younger
I would be a post apocalyptic
Warrior princess of words
I would tear it all up,
Rip the world up by its heart
And watch it drip in my hands.
I will still tear it all up;
I will poison its flippant heart
One beat at a time,
Coffee cup after cup after cup.
And when it falls over from apathy,
No one will be the wiser.

WRITER'S BLOCK

Maybe I don't have it in me, the way you do.
Maybe it just sits there, teasing me,
Waiting to consume me.
I can almost feel it, and I ache.
The unbearable unreachable.
It's grinning at me as I suffer.
I sit in the dark with visions that taunt me,
My fingers heavy with intent,
As it all spills out.

A pin dropped hard,
Broken by a cold grey
floor.
And deafening was the
tiny noise
As it stopped my heart.

WEE HOURS

I am outside with my dogs.
Cars on the highway nearby, racing,
Far away from here.
The crickets chirp monotonously, in complacent tune
With the drudge of my heart.
There are no stars in this night sky,
Just a sliver of a smirking moon that beams
With irrelevant delight.
When the sun is soon up, I will sleep at last,
Fitful, with a burning dread inside my dreams.

FOLD

I need quiet,
For thoughts to cease to exist.
Black skies drenched in stars,
The caress of cold air
Along my cheek.
I need my heart to have a slow and steady beat,
My dreams not remembered.
The tumultuous wreck of life
My eyes wake to feast upon each day
With bleak voracity
Siphons joy from my veins,
Breaks my heart,
I fold.

SNAKEPIT

I wonder what he's doing today—
Rolling over in bed, humming a song
Playing on his phone
Everyday just a dream
For all of us
And he's just going about his business
He sits on the edge of his bed,
The edge of my deep green sea
I would push him into blankets
As he clings like fire to me
"Wait until you hear this song"
Wait until you see what I have
Wait until you open your eyes
And the stars are all behind me
I'm the moon inside
Dark light blinding
And here we are, now
Deep in the snake pit, writhing
A sigh heaved deep
The sun is on its way up
I'm as giddy as Christmas,
And I can't believe my luck
The slush is slowly melting
Muddy water in the drains
Flowing down and hard
Into antiseptic brains
One last kiss before I go
Fingers cold pressed
Hard onto me
He is humming again now,
Smiling in his dreams.

SKYDIVE

How to know that I love you so
When any second, I will leave
Any careless word, I will jump
From your 50th story window
Plummeting
The crash so much more
Wonderful
Than another ending.

THE GIFT

The resentful demons
That reside so
Spitefully
Inside your pretty head;
Poor things!
How could they be wrestled?
How could they be heard by your unsympathetic ears?
Happiness is but a sparkling veneer
Like the shiny teeth that smile
Ready to bite those too close
Who see their clenched model poise.
Banishment,
What freedom!
Disloyalty, the gift that gave way
To clarity
To redirection
To love.

IF YOU MUST KNOW

All I want to do
Is drag you away
And do things
That will make you ask me
If I am crazy.
But if you must know—
Yes.

CHAINS

I am guarded by ghosts
Phantoms of pain, that cut to the quick.
I sit idle, watching.
The game plays out.
I stay silent, knowing
You wouldn't hear my chains
If I rattled them.
My tell-tale heart
Trembles
Within these haunted walls.

HURRICANE

My heart whirled and sloshed and battered
My ribcage with stormy excitement.
You will always be my hurricane.
I will batten down the hatches.
Giant waves may try to drown us.
I will grab your hand in slow motion
With salt water eyes
That sting like rabid bees
To save you,
As long as you don't let go.
Sometimes I let go,
A current grabs me, breaks me away.
Do you look for me?
Can you see me in the stormy swirls
Beneath the waves?
Sometimes it is easier to come up for air,
Than to keep holding my breath.

WORDS THAT NEVER EMIT SOUND

Heartbeats hammer hollow
Within this scared chest
There is dissonance;
Erratic notes and noise.
Static that will drown out
Every feeling.
What I hear is not a language.
It is pain upon pain upon fear.
Layers and layers, years and years.
Who is the glacier?
Me or you?
You are ice so solid
Too frozen to move.
I am ice so cold
I burn to hold.
Time will erode us
Until we melt into apathy
Potential drowned
By the nothingness of the sea.

SORRY

Sometimes you cannot say
Enough sorries
To make it matter
Sometimes
You think you are right
But it is your own heart
That you shatter.

HELPFUL

It helps
To be beautiful
To speak loudly
To have a face
That you do not mind
Showing
To have eyes that will
Bravely creep from behind
Messy hair
That will look upon the world
Without fear
It helps
To have not been riddled
With poisonous tongue lashings
Your entire life
It helps
To know
If how you feel
Is how you really feel
Or how you've been programmed to feel
Or to know
If how you react
Is appropriate
Or accurate
Or how
Your brain is protecting itself
It helps
To have words
That will flow when you call them
Sometimes there is a creek
Sometimes there is a river
Sometimes there is a dam
That breaks
That will spill into the ocean

SLUDGE

Plague heavy sick
Black sludge, barely moving
Sinking back out of the depths
You always swim out of
There is tepid hope
Lingering in the shadows
But until it steps out from behind
The fear that embraces you
Each step will be slower
Each breath more labored
The sky just a bit more grey

SNAKE

Pitiful venomous snake
You lie in a heap
Waiting on your prey
In a trailer park
The best you can do
Is not even
Mediocre
Poison drips from your fangs
You swallow it gleefully in gulps
You shiver at the wind
Reminding you again
You are more than fallible
Every misstep and mistake
Is imprinted in your DNA
You will keep biting
To drown out the failure
Barely treading water
As you writhe through every
Misery
Over and over

BRAVERY

Some people are brave.
They go knowingly into losing battles.
My words are the shiniest swords.
They shimmer as they slit your throat.
I carry you on horseback, to a suitable burial ground,
And still you try to stand up.
I nudge you with a lazy fingertip,
And watch as you wobble.
I am saddened and satisfied with such an exchange.
Your heart remains inside your chest.

DREAMS

I would tell you
How my heart swells
When I touch your skin
And your eyes
Light me on fire
You tell me something simple
When my insides are a tornado
And there is instant calm,
A silent sea
Butterflies wreak havoc within me
When you say my name
And I never mean it
When I say
"Don't tickle me!"
When you hold me
And I feel
I am as close to you
As I can possibly get
You pull me ever closer
And I am full of dreams

WAR

Destroy cities
Drink blood
Fire shots
Forget yourself
Forget fear
Shout louder
Aim higher
Claim peace
Shatter souls
Eat hearts
With a smile

BLOOM

Music is surging in me
My soul lifts off concrete
And dances as though in rain
Beneath a scorching sky
It takes more blood
To pump these words through
More string to sew
These words together true
Everything so delicate
Fairies in the palms of our hands
Wings aflutter
Everything precious
Susceptible
To one wrong move
We will bloom
Burst through the dirt
Leave our roots buried
And rush to the sun

DISDAIN

Disdain is a potent flavor
It percolates through my veins
And I see nothing
Shiny
New
Innovative
Wise
It is the same
Mundane
Cliché
Horse shit
Except
With a colorful background

TIPTOE

Happy
Sun shining dark
Revel and dance in warmth.
Sigh, smile, sigh.
Consistency, a concept
As foreign as Neptune.
Timid feet tremble in the dirt
In solidarity.

SMUG

It is not a poem
That you spit out so breezily
Like a reward for likes that placate
Your mock inflated ego.
Each one is a bland romance at best.
You will replace it next week
With another girl
Another song
Another beer
Another artistic endeavor with a vagina—
How inventive and insightful, oh poet!
I will sit back and be smug because my poems
Have more than one word per
Line.

LIGHT

I want to lure you
Into the cave
You are afraid of
Hold you steady
In the dark
You feel the jagged edges
As you crawl to me
Stumbling,
Bleeding,
I will lick your wounds
I will be your light.

OYSTER

I am set for life with a brooding heart,
My angels black and fallen.
My coffee cold, my legs closed tight,
I feel most things appalling.
A crescent in the sky,
Gives a wink of his eye,
All-knowing clouds, tease and bluster.
To know, out there,
Maybe somewhere,
There is someone who might muster
A strength unseen,
To open me,
This rough and dirty oyster.

FACE SWAP

Can you face swap
A spider and a moth
Are the wings so thick
And the eyes so many?
Is there truth in sameness
Despite a docile package?
There is survival in blood
And in flight.

WEB

I am tangled in a web
Of empathy and anger
Suffocating from my own
Heartstrings
Ignoring warnings
I know better
How do I free myself
And do better
I have always
Fed the spider
I need to slip this web
Fly away from the sound
Of clinking fangs
And hunger pains
Sigh relief into the sunset
Knowing I will see it
Again.

REASONS TO DROWN

When you are walking wounded
You feel the wind in your bones
Darkness is hovering
And it is your home
It chides you for moving so slowly
For crawling
With no means
Of momentum
It scolds you loudly
Amongst the stones
For not being better
But the moon sees all
And holds out her hand
Lighting your way
You keep moving
Deliberately
Dreading the day
You no longer see stars
Or feel the wind
You will look
For reasons to drown
Again

SEAFARING

I am sorry
I apologized
When you were
Being an asshole
Cruelty has always been
Your strong suit
I am sorry
That I somehow
Felt responsible
For your feelings
It is not my job
To incessantly
Smooth the waters
For a ship that has sailed
My waters were rough
I fought tooth and nail
Despite you leaving me behind to
Drown
I am grateful now
I learned to swim
My lungs strong and full
Now
I can breathe
For long periods of time
Underwater
And when I come up for air
Some people still love me

CONFESSIONS

My words are coming down on me,
Pelting me like rain
And once those words seep out of me
Confessions here again
Anything conjured of a memory
A song
A flittered heartbeat many years ago,
Now
Then
When?
No one knows.
Every sliver of feeling
A note on the piano
Loud and long
Hear the hollow of the tone
How does it make you feel now?

I see the word
"poverty"
And think it is the word
"poetry"
And either way
I am not wrong

STRESSED IS JUST DESSERTS
SPELLED BACKWARDS

I always want the grit
With the rain
The cold
The hard pavement
The urban movement
The flush of the struggle
The joy of small things
Camaraderie
Unity
The fight
Or flight
Because appreciation
Comes in small packages
When you feel you are
Undeserving
The just desserts
More fleeting
With more meaning
What is the reward
For a beige life
Handcrafted, mass produced,
Overpriced
The same smile
Promoting perfection
As a lifestyle rather than an affectation

AT A RED LIGHT

Smug male writer
"Yeah I liked some of your poems.
Let's get a drink when you're in town."
Even though I know
He already has a muse
Every woman
Is a different poem
I'm just a mystery
Because I'm in Texas
I text back politely at a red light,
While rolling my eyes.

A NIGHTMARE

I've been crying for 100 years, in a river of blood.
My fingers shriveled and shredded,
Clawing for air.
Choking on this liquid metal that soaks my lungs,
Pauses my breath.
Gasping.
I am singular, and no sound comes out.
There is no one to scream to.
Even the trees are silent.
I keep splashing, red and desperate.
I only think—
Relief,
Relief,
Relief.

Anxiety
Was the reason
You left me
And it has never done me
A bigger favor

ADULTHOOD

"I'll have no soul left when I finish this rat race,"
She said.
"I will wither away,
Dry up,
Crumble like ashes."
"We all do," I explained.
I paused to listen for my own heartbeat.
Silence.

AUTUMN

Crows fly in sunshine
Early morning setting in
Leaves so crisp they break our hearts
As this day leers and beckons
Clandestine chill
And fervid crunch
Souls shoot through a darker sky
Joy comes soon through wicked dance
And tears fall from our eyes

BATTLESHIP

Sometimes I do not like my own voice,
Even when I am not speaking.
What do I have to say?
This battleship is not unique.
But despite the same scars
as other ships,
this ship still sails.
I put my ear to the shell that
Whispers the ocean to me,
And I float.
My voice may haunt me
Through the waves and darkness
Of every night
But perhaps it washes up on your shore
Inside a bottle that you open
In hopes that you are not alone.

BETTER ME THAN YOU

Feelings are monsters crawling inside of me.
I must keep them in chains, locked up
And away from the general public.
People know they're in there—
They want to take a peek.
Or throw a rock.
Or feel around for them in the dark.
Poke at them with a stick.
My poor monsters.
They only want to just BE.
If they can be contained, for awhile, they may just go
back to where they came from.
Their mere presence could incite a riot.
Occasionally one escapes.
It is mass hysteria.
These monsters don't know how to conduct
themselves.
It is all wild screams, a thirst for blood.
It is better to stay as far away from them as you can.
I try to stay away from them if I can. But they know
I hold the keys to their cage and sometimes they rattle
And rattle until I let them out if only to stop the noise.
Eventually I crawl back into the cage with them.
Better they eat me alive than someone else.

COCO

These wounds may never heal.
There is no precision with which to close my heart.
It is gaping and would howl if it could.
I ache in such silence,
But I would howl if I could.

Now I know how they will all look when they go,
How tiny their breaths, the whites of their eyes
With a resigned heave, she lay to one side.
My love, my heart-- how she tried.

CONSPIRACY

My throat and tongue are locked,
Entwined, in a silent conspiracy.
They hold my shy heart hostage.
The words she would send up the pipes!
If only they would let her.

FILTH

nothing is important
we are all

b l e e d i n g

red insignificance
mopping the floor with us

s m e a r e d

what was once necessary
for perseverance
now bubbles and clots
dries up

c l i n g i n g

to irrelevant
filth

HEADLIGHTS

I should have taken the hints
I froze, a deer in headlights
Tiptoeing over lava
I wanted to go to your outstretched hand,
I was fearful of a sudden move
And now I dream
Of a sudden move.

I GET TIRED OF THE BUTS AND WHAT IFS

I am chugging coffee
I am ignoring the patriarchy
I am ignoring those that say they love us and yet
Deny the trauma
That was thrust upon us
Because we didn't want to
Talk to 3 different police departments
Or be told
What we experienced
Didn't happen, it wasn't like that
Or sit and drive ourselves crazy
Wondering if
Despite the fear or the pain
Maybe
Just maybe
He is right
And what you felt
Was, (as of course, all women are)
Irrational
Being fondled in your sleep
Is kindness?
Innocence?
You are 15 and think this boy is cute
So you should
Just let it happen
I loathe that I feel GRATEFUL
To someone
For bringing me home when I asked
Because I didn't want to do what he asked
I didn't want to make out with him even
But the rest? I said, "No I need to go home."
He took me home and kissed me again.

And I didn't want it but you have to write it off,
Because at least he didn't rape you
How many girls say yes
Just so they don't have to fight it off?
It isn't okay.
Why is it such an affront
To be sure everyone is cool
With what's happening?
Why is it OFFENSIVE?
Is it too offensive to your manhood
That you might be told no?
So you don't even ask,
And everything about her movements are
Begrudging, and yet
You enjoy yourselves
Thoroughly
Because you are basically
Using a woman to masturbate with.
If women admitting their trauma
In solidarity
Is so disgusting to people
Then perhaps they should
Act accordingly
And not inflict trauma,
Teach their children
To not inflict trauma
To speak and listen
Rather than condemn
Without skipping a beat
Because it is an inconvenience
Or they might have to look at someone
They don't even know in real life
Differently
Even though they are looking at women
They know and love,
Differently.

NORMAL

I am torn
In one trillion directions
I am happy
I am sad
I am picking myself apart
Scratching at the seams
As anxiety eats me alive
A starving animal on the inside
I am in love
I am grieving
Living tragedies
I can't get close enough to the end
I am broken
I am nerves
Scrambled eggs
My brain
Just breathe again

LIT

The fumes of gas lit
Horse shit
Are heavy in the air
To intoxicate
As we simmer
In our rage
Division
Ego
Walking dysfunction
Find the bridge you need to cross
Keep your matches in your pocket
You aren't there yet—
There may be another bridge

TEACUPS

I will never beg for
The twinkle in those eyes.
How to differentiate a kind word
With a shove on the swing
And boasts of brutality
To tiny teacup hearts?
Do we lay blame
And keep ghosts clanking
In our brains
Making us both prisoners?
I would so love to erase them
From every cell
That ever ached.

YOU SEE HOW IT IS

Tiny death, you come to me.
I command it, finger the black lace,
As me, as you.
Muscles contracting, expanding,
Gripping, deep—there is no when.
I sit you down
And you see how it is,
Breathless, waiting in the darkness.
Aloof, bold and voracious,
Hiding the heart.

PHOTOSYNTHESIS

You will get along fine
You always do
The worst has come and gone
You are still standing
You only have to
Take a deep breath
Put one foot in front of the other
You cannot let terror
Wilt you like a flower
You are a
Magnanimous bloom
Seek the sun
Feel your tendrils
Expanding and growing
Stretch to the sky
Keep
Going

SWIM

I will
Swim harder
Through
The smirks
The sighs
The rolling eyes
The condescension
I will fly
On waves
Recreate
A word for every
Apprehension
The blood will flow
Apropos
From my pen
And that is when
My so called friend
You will see
My face again

NIGHT VISION

I crave you like the moon
Every night
I must see you
Silky breaths
Cradle my skin
As you light the way
With your fingertips

CREATURE COMFORT

Overwhelmed and overworked.
No beach in sight.
And still, no
Birth control,
Food stamps,
Insulin,
Health insurance,
Humanity,
For you.
There are devils in their smiles as
They enunciate a God they use to
Line their power and their pockets.
The same God who would cringe at
Their wild lies, infidelities,
And apathetic disdain.
What will cushion the blow to civilization
As it is systematically destroyed
With a golden sledgehammer?
Another Xanax pushed by the doctor
Whose copay is the same
As a week's worth of groceries?
A vacation you pay for by payday loan?
The love that they seek to electrocute out of you?
A body you are finally comfortable in
That makes it almost passable to murder?
The roof above your head that gets smaller
And more expensive by the year?
Will you lap it up as your soul is stretched
And air becomes a creature comfort?
Maybe when the ice really melts, our hearts will.

UNIVERSE

You are air
You are light
You touch everything
On me
My skin
Its depths
Shudder
Turning
To syrup
Slow and sweet

COCOON

We could build a cocoon
In this room
Me and you.
Entwined,
Our butterfly legs
Everywhere,
Together.
We will emerge
From this chrysalis
That has kept us
In perpetual
Metamorphosis;
We will fly away
Beautiful,
Opaque,
Marvelous.

PREVAIL

Within the waves of dust and debris that once
Cluttered my sight,
Our souls, the lives we trudge through,
There is a softness that prevails.
Cushions we fall upon,
Sighs that can escape and swim
Through our own relief.
Breathe!
See the sun peeking from beneath
Purple clouds, the pink sky,
Everything new and trying!
I am heartened.

THE WAIT

I feel togetherness in words that flow like glowing lights
From my smiling mouth.
My heartbeat hangs in the balance
When I wait for your reply.

ECHOES

I relax hearing a wind storm
Banging the screen against the window
The world is at unrest
And will blow us all away

Each breath and good thought
Tonight
Is challenging

But here I sit
Covered in four-legged
Unconditional love.

Who needs
Anyone's opinions?
Never did I ask you
For a detailed
Characterization of my soul
Or for you to
Rate mine against yours
Or to hear, "at least I..."

Every human has
Their marks against them

The question is
What marks
Do you have going FOR you?

When you are a ball of tears
And worries
Remember!

You are sweet like Dr. Pepper
Wrapped in a cloud
You would help any soul
You were able
You are fiercely honest
You do everything you can
There is integrity in your veins

And most importantly
You try
Even when once
You would have stopped.

Those cruel echoes in the night do not matter.
You will wake up to sun and smiles and silence.

SUPERGLUE

a million words under wraps
my lips set out to give me away
they are sewn together and yet bursting at the seams
pushed further and further to the edge
with every heartbeat.
my tongue savors the sweetness of every syllable
ready to slide them out
they dance and twitch and tingle
as i shiver

THAT'S WHAT YOU GET FOR THINKING

Betrayal comes even with laughter
   that brings you tears.
Joy that is innocent,
   that you thought would never harsh.
You thought all of the secrets
   and confessions and vulnerability
   and rawness would bind you like glue.
You thought decades mattered.
You thought effort mattered.
You thought self sacrifice
   and unconditional love mattered.
You thought being there
   when no one else was mattered.
You thought same-named mothers mattered.
You thought spiral notebooks mattered.
You thought love and loss and Klonopin mattered.
You thought self-awareness
   and self-consciousness mattered.
You thought Happy Tuesday cheesecakes mattered.
You thought apologies
   for missteps and mistakes mattered.
You thought communication, understanding,
   and sharing the same brain mattered.
Perhaps all of that did
But you did not.

THE BALLET

Your bloodstream gone cold
You wait with pitiful words that do not echo
The shadows lurk
And creep over your thoughts
So gingerly
Phantom ballerinas
Who repeat repeat repeat
Wholeheartedly
There is not enough voice
Despite internal noise
You plea in silence
Dark reverie

HEAVY

Wordless for once
Hiding in a grey haze
Dark days scald
No epiphany
These are heavy steps
That we now walk
But they must trample the silence and misery
Even ever so slightly

WHITE FLAG

You crushed her, a tiny blue robin egg of a girl.
She fell in your palm,
And you clamped it shut.
Always hovering, the threat of shutdown imminent.
How do you pump those lungs full of air again?
She may never breathe on her own.
One day she grew too big for your hand.
So you stepped on her.
Smashed her to the floor.
Somehow she stuck to your shoe
And hung on for dear life
Until you scraped her off;
Just a piece of chewed up, old gum.
Flung by the wayside, she clung to anything else.
Delicate melodies helped her float away,
Rare kind words from strangers,
Regenerated the heart and lungs
That still hung like tattered white flags inside of her.

THE PASSENGER

I try to never panic
She always comes back
Even when I am disconnected
Floating through the sunshine
And many tragedies
She is hanging back
Brewing and stewing
A true bad bitch
She's got me
And when she finally saunters in
Sometimes a little "whatever whatever"
She tells me to move over
Always her passenger.

VACATION

Eventually
You will be angry
You were run out of town
Even though
You packed your own bags

SELF-SERVING

I stand in line to criticize
I rub my arms with lotion
To moisturize the flab
As I stare, I see tedious, youthful freckles
Dotting my skin like a landscape.
Flab yes, but young and purposeful skin,
Able-bodied.
My arms do what they are meant to do.
Push away, fight back, crawl, reach things.
My legs the same, my heart the same.
Can I feel happy with this body because it serves me?
These arms grab vodka when I need them to.
These arms grab hugs when I need them to.

NEVERMIND

What do you feel?
Rhetorical
I want it real, but—
Oh wow, nevermind
Sorry you asked.
Shut it down
One word answers
It is all "too much"
Life
Sorrows
Worries
Woes
Annoying-
A slowly dripping faucet
You cover your ears from
And then
When there is minute joy
A smile
A random pirouette
One tiny beam in the darkness
The door slams
Louder

SUCKERPUNCH

Sometimes I feel
The essence of my existence
Is like
Blood in the kidneys.

EXQUISITE

Let's listen to music in bed
While you tell me your secrets
I trace your back with my fingertips
Underneath the blankets
I want to hear you breathing
Not quite asleep, almost dreaming
I have never been so
Exquisitely
Terrified

HELIUM

I huff the scent of you on my pillow like gasoline,
And it sets me on fire.
You make every cell in my body feel full of helium,
Fizzy and bubbly, straight to my head.

DECADENCE

Dreams of tiny deaths
We are so close
With a predilection
For secret sunrises
Awash in fire
Every cell melts
In unparalleled
Decadence

COLOR

No concept of big or small
The silence consumes us
I am
Hiding
Flying
Fumbling
The sky is purple
And my heart pounds
Can we flee what is coming for us all
If we do not move a muscle?
Your grey smile crumbles when you whisper
I only feel in color

BULLFIGHT

I thought I needed some Hemingway motherfucker
To drag me out of this wreckage
Kicking and screaming
And he would love every red-blooded
Heart-throbbing moment of it
I would tread frightfully, and he would hear me,
Clip clock clacking, indignant,
He would wave his red flag,
He would taunt and tease me until I tire,
He would wear me down
Despite the dust behind my heels
And we would gore each other at the end
...but I didn't.
In the end, I am a sweet and smiling cow,
Doe eyed,
Wearing a wreath of flowers,
Soaking up the sun
In my meadow.
Love will tame the beast.

PANIC

I can be
An extremist
The loudest alarm
Choke on my own
Gasping breaths
Of side swept panic
I wish my dear brain
Had the fortitude
To always
Stay steady
Stay strong
Stay calm
But she must protect me
At all unreasonable costs
In many unreasonable ways
But this is all she knows
And I am happy
She still tries.

The End

ABOUT THE AUTHOR

Heather Blank is a silly goose who writes to survive.
She lives in Dallas, Texas, and has a deep appreciation
for music, pugs, cats, plants, and rum.

Contact/Inquiries:

fb: /heatherblankpoet
ig: @heatherblankpoet
email: heatherblankpoet@gmail.com

Made in the USA
Coppell, TX
18 August 2022

81562495R00059